to do about them. Over forty days, we step into God's work in the here and now – and in doing so we move from brokenness towards wholeness.

Our journey through Lent is one in which we seek inner transformation to be people of a new world, people who live by a vision of God's world, where all are created equal.

Our prayer is that this may be a time for you – whether by yourself, in community, or online – to see afresh the vision of God and truly join in making his promise of a world transformed a reality.

**Archbishop Justin Welby &
Archbishop Stephen Cottrell**

ACKNOWLEDGEMENTS

#LiveLent: Embracing Justice is the Church of England's theme for Lent 2022.

Both the Archbishop of Canterbury's 2022 Lent Book, *Embracing Justice* (SPCK), and this daily reflections booklet for adults have been written by **Isabelle Hamley**, Theological Adviser to the House of Bishops and formerly Chaplain to the Archbishop of Canterbury.

The Church House Publishing and the Church of England Communications teams would like to express their gratitude to SPCK Publishing for their willingness to collaborate to maximise the range of print and digital resources offered to churches, discussion groups and individuals this year. And we are most grateful to Isabelle Hamley for ensuring the close coordination across the resources by writing both the Lent book and these reflections based on it.

Details of the Lent book and the full range of resources to support this year's Lent theme can be found at **churchofengland.org/livelent**

CONTENTS

HOW TO USE THIS BOOKLET

#LiveLent: Embracing Justice invites us to examine our own lives truthfully, to see the world more deeply and to pray – for the church and the world far and near – that 'justice may roll down like waters, and righteousness like an ever-flowing stream' (Amos 5.24).

This booklet contains 40 reflections, each for one of the forty days in Lent, which begins on Ash Wednesday (which falls on 2 March in 2022) and ends on Easter Eve (Saturday 16 April in 2022), plus one for Easter Day. You can use it on its own, but my hope is that those who are also reading the Archbishop of Canterbury's Lent Book 2022, *Embracing Justice* (SPCK) either individually or as part of a discussion group will find it helpful, too.

For each week (starting on a Sunday from Week 1 onwards) there is:

- A **theme** which corresponds to the chapters of the 2022 Lent book
- A **brief introduction** to the theme and readings for the week
- A **challenge** linked to the theme which suggests a practical action you might take.

Each week we follow a different thread through the many stories of justice in the Bible to explore how God works with humanity to bring justice, wholeness and salvation to all.

For each day (Monday to Saturday) there are daily reflections which offer:

· A **theme**
· A **picture**
· A **short passage from the Bible**
· A **short reflection** on the theme and reading
· A **simple prayer**.

Finally, there are a range of suggestions for **Going Further**.

There is also a version of the daily challenge for children and families available in the accompanying booklet *#LiveLent: Embracing Justice – For Kids*. This offers a weekly reading and prayer, together with a daily challenge to help all ages explore how we can live well together.

The booklet will be accompanied by daily social media posts from Ash Wednesday to Easter Day, together with a wide range of video and other free digital resources for individuals, groups and churches available via **churchofengland.org/livelent**

JUSTICE IN CREATION

The Genesis creation accounts paint an idyllic picture of humanity all created equal, made in the image of God, in their diversity and difference, enjoying the gifts of God's abundance. How did it all go so wrong?

Action for the week

This week, pray every morning that God would help you see his image in every person you meet.

In the evening, spend a few minutes reviewing the day. Who did you meet God in? Who did you struggle with?

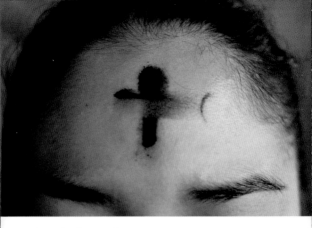

Ash Wednesday

TURNING FROM AND TURNING TO

Read: Isaiah 55.1-11

> *Seek the Lord while he may be found, call upon him while he is near; let the wicked forsake their way, and the unrighteous their thoughts; let them return to the Lord, that he may have mercy on them, and to our God, for he will abundantly pardon.*

Ash Wednesday is a day of turnings. A day when we turn inwards and examine our lives; a day when we turn from the depth of winter to waiting for Easter. And a day when we choose to turn away from sin and towards new life.

This isn't something we do on our own. Christians all over the world use this time as a line in the sand, a yearly reminder of both our frailty, and God's grace.

The fact that we do this together, rather than on our own, reminds us that it isn't just our personal lives that need transforming, but that of our communities, countries and entire world. On Ash Wednesday, and in Lent, we lament the brokenness of the whole world, its sin, inequality and injustice, and we long for God's intervention to come and teach us what justice, peace and freedom truly look like.

Prayer

Loving God, we bring ourselves, our churches, and our world before you: we ask that you show us, alone and together, how to turn and walk in your ways. Amen.

Thursday after Ash Wednesday
JUSTICE IN CREATION

Read: Genesis 1.24-31

> *Then God said, 'Let us make humankind in our image, according to our likeness ... '*
> *So God created humankind in his image, in the image of God he created them; male and female he created them.*

Everyone knows when something unfair happens to them. It is as if human beings have an in-built sensor that tracks injustice, which is strange because injustice is far more widespread than perfectly fair environments!

What do we mean by 'it's not fair'? Maybe it is a cry of suffering – or maybe sometimes a cry of entitlement? Or maybe it is something deep within us that reaches back to a vision of the world as it should be, where all human beings are created equal, made in the image of God, and difference does not lead to hierarchy and value judgements. A creation where human beings' relationships with one another, with God, and with the whole of creation is balanced, right and fair, with no exploitation, no barriers and no hierarchies.

Listening to our cries of unfairness helps us discover the world we long for – and ask whether our hopes and longings are shaped by God's principles in creation.

Prayer

Generous God, teach us to treasure your image in one another and share your gifts of generosity and abundance in love for the world and its people. Amen.

Friday after Ash Wednesday
WHEN GOOD GOES BAD

Read: Genesis 3.1-19

> *They heard the sound of the Lord God walking in the garden at the time of the evening breeze, and the man and his wife hid themselves from the presence of the Lord God … The man said, 'The woman whom you gave to be with me, she gave me fruit from the tree, and I ate.' Then the Lord God said to the woman, 'What is this that you have done?' The woman said, 'The serpent tricked me, and I ate.'*

Life in the garden was idyllic, but it wasn't good enough. Human beings long for power and control, and in this story, they want to control right and wrong, good and bad. They want to define ethics for themselves, not in relationship with God.

And so everything goes wrong: the harmony of creation starts to tear and fragment. People hide from God. Cooperation turns to blame. Difference becomes a barrier. Natural equality turns to dominance. The easy abundance of the garden turns into hard, thankless work to eke out a living. All relationships, between people and God, each other and with nature are disturbed. Every story that follows will exemplify this breakdown of relationship, and its horrendous impact on the most vulnerable, and on the land itself.

How has this story played out in your own life?

Prayer

God of forgiveness, we bring our broken lives and our broken world before you: mend our relationship with you, with one another, and with the world you gifted us. Amen.

MAKING SENSE OF A BROKEN WORLD

Read: Matthew 7.1-5

> *Jesus said, 'Why do you see the speck in your neighbour's eye, but do not notice the log in your own eye? Or how can you say to your neighbour, "Let me take the speck out of your eye", while the log is in your own eye?'*

The biblical accounts of creation affirm that all human beings are equally loved, equally valuable, equally worthy. But they also say human beings are equally flawed, all responsible for a broken world. The first reaction of the humans after eating the forbidden fruit was to blame – the other, the serpent, even God!

In the face of injustice, our first reaction is often, 'It's X's fault!' We point the finger. Discerning truth and speaking truth to power are important. Yet Scripture reminds us that truth cannot be found through blame alone. Truth starts with us and our own failings.

Owning up to our part in the brokenness of the world means that we do not stand in condemnation, but stand with others who are condemned, and know that they, like us, are in need of grace. This truth prevents us from dividing the world between goodies and baddies. It forces us to see people as people.

Prayer

God of truth, help me to see where my thoughts, words and actions hurt, damage and maim your people and your creation; and to accept your offer of transformation. Amen.

EXODUS AND LIBERATION

Exodus is a great story of justice: a people oppressed, whose very life is at stake, are rescued by God's intervention, and led through the desert to form a new community, centred on God, defined by his justice and compassion.

Action for the week

Try and watch or read the news every day. Is there one group, or one person's pain or oppression which stands out? Can you think of one practical action you could take to stand in solidarity – a letter, an email, a donation?

Monday, Week 1
FROM GUESTS TO SLAVES

Read: Exodus 1.8-22

> *Now a new king arose over Egypt, who did not know Joseph. He said to his people, 'Look, the Israelite people are more numerous and more powerful than we. Come, let us deal shrewdly with them, or they will increase and, in the event of war, join our enemies and fight against us and escape from the land.' Therefore they set taskmasters over them to oppress them with forced labour.*

The people of Israel, newly settled in Egypt, find that being Joseph's protégés does not stand the test of time. They once were guests of a powerful man, but quickly they are seen as strangers and their life and vigour become threatening. People start talking about 'them'. They are no longer friends, neighbours, partners. They are the 'other' – the ones to blame, the ones to fear, the ones who don't belong. And once they are no longer seen as equals, sharing humanity, the door opens for them to be mistreated, enslaved, and, in the end, exterminated as all their boy babies are killed.

Injustice does not start with actions, it starts with words and thoughts. It starts with looking at another person and seeing them as less than equal, less worthy of life and love and dignity. And as words are shared, actions follow. Is there anyone you speak about as 'other'?

Prayer

Loving God, challenge me when I talk of anyone as less than myself, and help me speak up when others speak in ways that diminish or disparage people who differ from them. Amen.

Tuesday, Week 1
HEARING, SEEING, REMEMBERING

Read: Exodus 2.23-3.8a

> *After a long time the king of Egypt died. The Israelites groaned under their slavery, and cried out. Out of the slavery their cry for help rose up to God. God heard their groaning, and God remembered his covenant with Abraham, Isaac, and Jacob. God looked upon the Israelites, and God took notice of them.*

Oppression and injustice are not just words, they are harsh realities for real people of flesh and blood. Under Pharaoh's rule, the people of Israel cry out in pain. The story does not say that they cry out to God. They do not argue, demand or reason. They simply groan in pain and anguish, and it is to this cry of pain that God responds. God will bring justice and liberation, but first God hears their cry and God sees their pain.

It is compassion that moves God to act in power. When God hears and sees, God 'remembers' his covenant. In other words, the people's pain puts a claim on the one who sees and hears. Who else had seen and heard but not been moved to compassion? Who else had seen and heard but refused to accept that they could not be a bystander and had to act?

Prayer

Patient God, open my eyes to see the people I usually ignore and listen to those I pass by, and open my heart to be changed by their stories. Amen.

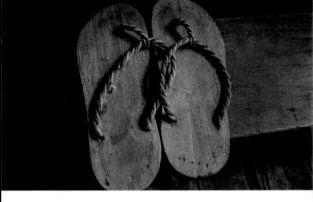

THE GOD WHO TRANSFORMS
PART 1 – MOSES

Read: Exodus 2.11-15 and 3.7-22

> 'So come, I will send you to Pharaoh to bring my people, the Israelites, out of Egypt.' But Moses said to God, 'Who am I that I should go to Pharaoh, and bring the Israelites out of Egypt?' He said, 'I will be with you; and this shall be the sign for you that it is I who sent you: when you have brought the people out of Egypt, you shall worship God on this mountain.'

Moses had the best preparation. A Hebrew brought up in the house of Pharaoh, he should have had confidence to challenge the status quo. The problem is, Moses had learnt too well, and come to think like Pharaoh. His first foray into trying to do justice led him to kill an Egyptian and flee to the desert. His first attempt failed, and he realised how small he was.

But failure is never the last word with God. Moses is invited to learn to do justice God's way: giving Pharaoh multiple chances to change willingly; putting worship first, ahead of any other consideration; being aware of his own frailty. As Moses grows as a leader, slowly the harsh, perverted justice of Egypt makes way for justice rooted in compassion, humility and reliance on God's initiative.

Prayer

Transforming God, we thank you for Moses, for his frailties and failures, and his growth in grace and holiness. May we, too, be ready to be changed by the fire of your presence. Amen.

THE GOD WHO TRANSFORMS
PART 2 – PHARAOH

Read: Exodus 5.1-14

> Afterwards Moses and Aaron went to Pharaoh and said, 'Thus says the Lord, the God of Israel, "Let my people go, so that they may celebrate a festival to me in the wilderness." ' But Pharaoh said, 'Who is the Lord, that I should heed him and let Israel go? I do not know the Lord, and I will not let Israel go.'

Pharaoh is a king, often considered a god. In the logic of Egypt, he has no equal. How can some lowly Hebrew come and give him a message from some unknown God? Pharaoh's whole world is challenged. He cannot agree to the Hebrews' request without accepting that he himself is neither god nor ruler over all.

He does not hear or see the people and their pain. To see and hear the pain his actions are causing would force him to compassion, and compassion would challenge the logic of his whole empire. Compassion does not hoard resources, does not exploit others for one's own benefit. Compassion threatens Egypt's structures, and Pharaoh responds in the only way that he knows: by making the people's lives even harder. Pharaoh is invited to open himself to God, but ultimately, the transformation proves too threatening and costly, and he refuses.

Prayer

Holy God, we confess that we often hold on to our power, our possessions and our sins. Soften our hearts to hear your call that we may love you, and our neighbour, more deeply. Amen.

THE GOD WHO TRANSFORMS
PART 3 – ISRAEL

Read: Exodus 16.1-26

> *Then the Lord said to Moses, 'I am going to rain bread from heaven for you, and each day the people shall go out and gather enough for that day … On the sixth day, when they prepare what they bring in, it will be twice as much as they gather on other days.'*

Israel *thought* they were ready - to get out, leave Egypt, start a new life. But the logic and ways of Egypt still clung to them. They may be physically free, but their minds were still captive to Egypt's logic of scarcity and hoarding. If they took this thinking with them into the Promised Land, what kind of society would they build? Would fear lead them to exploit others in their turn? Would anxiety lead them to reproduce Egypt's obsession with productivity?

God's answer takes Israel through the desert, into the very heart of scarcity. In a place where there is nothing, they learn to live differently, getting what is needed for today, enough for every person, but never more than enough. Never hoarding for tomorrow the bread another needs today. The people's imagination of what they need is reshaped to care for every member, generously and equally.

What are you tempted to hoard?

Prayer

Generous God, help us to learn the difference between need and desire, and to refrain from taking tomorrow the bread that belongs to a neighbour today. Amen.

REMEMBERING EGYPT

Read: Exodus 12.21-32

> 'When you come to the land that the Lord will give you, as he has promised, you shall keep this observance. And when your children ask you, "What do you mean by this observance?" you shall say, "It is the passover sacrifice to the Lord, for he passed over the houses of the Israelites in Egypt, when he struck down the Egyptians but spared our houses." '

Another challenging character in Exodus is Pharaoh's daughter. In rescuing the baby Moses she defies her father with one single act of compassion that will bring Egypt to its knees. She collapses the easy caricature of Egyptians as 'enemies'. She, an Egyptian, also must be seen and heard. Indeed, the ritual with which Israel is instructed to remember the night of their liberation also stresses the cost of freedom in the loss of Egypt's children.

We often try to tame Exodus, read it selectively. To attend to the whole of Exodus is challenging, because it calls all of us to see and hear all around us, without prejudice or caricature, and bear witness. Exodus challenges us to examine how we seek justice: do we simply reproduce the patterns of thought and action of those we challenge? Or are we ready to be transformed by God's radical call to hold together justice and compassion for all?

Prayer

Loving God, inspire us to seek justice your way, driven by compassion for all, shaped by your holiness and ready to discover grace in the most unexpected places. Amen.

Week 2

BUILDING COMMUNITIES OF JUSTICE

The story of Exodus is not just a story of liberation. It goes hand in hand with the birth of a new community, shaped for justice and the flourishing of all with a set of laws for everyday living.

Action for the week

Think about your daily choices this week: who has produced your food, your clothes, who serves you while remaining invisible? Can you make one change in your buying or consumption habits to contribute to a better life for an invisible worker?

Monday, Week 2

WHY LAWS?

Read: Deuteronomy 10.12–11.1

> *So now, O Israel, what does the Lord your God require of you? Only to fear the Lord your God, to walk in all his ways, to love him, to serve the Lord your God with all your heart and with all your soul, and to keep the commandments of the Lord your God and his decrees that I am commanding you today, for your own well-being.*

The people are free, so what now? How can they organise themselves in ways that will enable all of them to stay free, rather than reproduce hierarchy and oppression? Scripture is pretty down-to-earth about it. The people need structures to help them live well. Laws are given to enable the boundaries for justice needed in the new community, to ensure that there is a space where all can flourish.

But laws on their own do not deliver a just society, they merely make it possible. It is the attitudes underlying the laws that matter: caring for the poor, the disadvantaged and the stranger, not primarily out of duty, but because they are people made in the image of God, loved by God. The laws of Scripture keep reinforcing that to do justice, to love our neighbour goes beyond duty: it is a response to God's love.

Prayer

God of justice and mercy, teach us to live well, to care for the widow, the orphan and the stranger, and love our neighbour as ourselves. Amen.

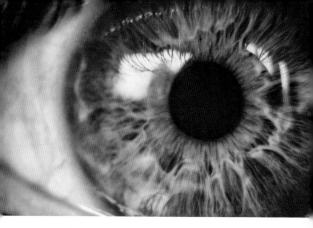

AN EYE FOR AN EYE?

Read: Leviticus 24.18-22
and Matthew 5.38-39

> *'You have heard that it was said,
> "An eye for an eye and a tooth for
> a tooth." But I say to you, Do not resist an
> evildoer. But if anyone strikes
> you on the right cheek,
> turn the other also.'*

'An eye for an eye, a tooth for a tooth' is a
well-known saying; it isn't obvious that it
comes directly from the Old Testament. What

do we make of it, given that Jesus famously commands a better way?

The saying comes in the context of a judicial system, rather than individual piety. 'An eye for an eye' establishes two essential principles: proportionality and judgement by a third party. When people are hurt, especially gravely hurt, they often want to lash out in revenge. This law ensures that justice is served rather than revenge – it limits retribution. 'An eye for eye' states that punishment must fit the crime, but never exceed it. Because judgement is arbitrated by a third party – the law – it affirms that justice is not just about individuals, but about the whole community looking after its members, witnessing to hurt and refusing to condone evil.

How can you tell whether you want justice or revenge?

Prayer

Holy God, root out the desire for revenge and the tendency to hold grudges from our hearts, and help us pursue justice so that all may flourish. Amen.

Wednesday, Week 2

A COMMUNITY OF RADICAL JUSTICE

Read: Leviticus 25.1-28

> *When you enter the land that I am giving you, the land shall observe a sabbath for the Lord. For six years you shall sow your field, and for six years you shall prune your vineyard, and gather in their yield; but in the seventh year there shall be a sabbath of complete rest for the land, a sabbath for the Lord.*

Leviticus isn't really anyone's favourite book. It usually gets quoted for strange laws we don't like. Yet at its heart is a vision so incredible, so radical, that we often shy away from it.

Chapter 25 sets out the principle of Jubilee for the people as they enter the Promised Land: the idea that work and productivity do not drive everything; that everyone and everything, including the land, must rest regularly.

Even more challenging, the year of Jubilee sees the erasure of debts, and a return of all land to original tribes and owners. Leviticus prescribes a reset of the economic and social clock every fifty years. A chance to say, the mistakes of the past do not have to define the future, and to remind the people not to hoard and accumulate riches that should be distributed fairly. The vision is breathtaking. No wonder we shy away from it.

Prayer

God of the poor and forgotten, help us stop our frantic striving for possessions. May we listen to your word, learn to rest, and embrace your offer of new life. Amen.

Thursday, Week 2

JUSTICE AS SHARED RESPONSIBILITY

Read: Exodus 19.1-8

> *Now therefore, if you obey my voice and keep my covenant, you shall be my treasured possession out of all the peoples. Indeed, the whole earth is mine, but you shall be for me a priestly kingdom and a holy nation.*

Out of Egypt, Israel is given a new identity, and with it, a vocation. They are the people of God, a 'treasured possession', their vocation, to embody God's way of life as a 'priestly kingdom' and 'a holy nation'. Kings used to be the ultimate arbiters of justice. But Israel is given no king. God is king, and the people, 'a priestly kingdom'. It is everyone's calling to uphold justice. Life cannot be fair, just or abundant unless a community as a whole seeks to live justly. Justice is not an individualistic enterprise, it is a communal vocation.

This is where things get difficult: in any community, different ideas of justice compete and individuals clash over rights and their version of the common good. Quickly, everyone pulls their own way, and common vocation falters. This is why Israel is called to be 'holy': to locate their unity not in consensus, but in imitation of God.

Prayer

Lord God, help us to seek justice together with all others in our communities – not just those we agree with, but seek the kind of justice that enables the flourishing of all. Amen.

SMALL PICTURE, BIG PICTURE

Read: Deuteronomy 4.5-14

> *See, just as the Lord my God has charged me, I now teach you statutes and ordinances for you to observe in the land that you are about to enter and occupy. You must observe them diligently, for this will show your wisdom and discernment to the peoples, who, when they hear all these statutes, will say, 'Surely this great nation is a wise and discerning people!'*

The law books of the Old Testament do two things. They give guidance for judicial matters – small scale, interpersonal, community level justice. They also give guidance on a broad canvas, for things that are not 'enforceable' as such: economic and social justice, constant directives to care for the poor, vulnerable and alien. These two aspects are intimately related: we can never be fully just individually unless we live within systems and societies that are just too.

I may seek to buy fairly-traded products, to be environmentally conscious, to give to charity. Nevertheless, my life is enmeshed in unjust systems that damage our planet and prop up gross inequalities within and between nations. To do justice is to address both, because neither is enough without the other.

How might you engage with these two aspects?

Prayer

God of all things, we pray that you would help us to shape our lives for justice, to speak up and witness to those things that are beyond our individual power to change. Amen.

WHEN JUSTICE FAILS

Read: Exodus 22.21-27

> If you take your neighbour's cloak in pawn, you shall restore it before the sun goes down; for it may be your neighbour's only clothing to use as cover; in what else shall that person sleep? And if your neighbour cries out to me, I will listen, for I am compassionate.

The Old Testament is nothing if not realistic. The community is given a vision for life, yet it also assumes that the vision will not be fully embodied. Specific laws are there because people break them. If there was no murder, theft or violence, there would be no need to legislate against them, or direct how to deal with them.

The laws implicitly say: injustice is a rule of life, it happens, and it must be taken seriously by the entire community.

Yet even with the best laws, sometimes, justice fails, through weakness, through ignorance, or deliberate fault, as in the words of confession. When justice fails, the words of Exodus take special poignancy: 'if your neighbour cries out to me, I will listen, for I am compassionate.' Injustice may be rampant, but it never has the final word.

Prayer

Merciful God, we recognise our failure to do justice, through the things we do and those we fail to do, through our words, and through our silence and complicity: cleanse and transform our lives. Amen.

JUSTICE AS ENCOUNTER

Justice in Scripture is always rooted in time, place and story. It is about people, and the image of God within them, an image damaged and distorted by sin – our own, and others'. This week we walk with Jesus as embraces those he meets.

Action for the week

Justice is about relationship, about a meeting of people, in their full humanity. Every day this week, try to speak to someone you would not normally speak with – someone you disagree with, or simply do not normally notice – and listen to their story, without interruption.

SEEING THE INVISIBLE

Read: Mark 5.21-34

> *Now there was a woman who had been suffering from haemorrhages for twelve years. She had endured much under many physicians, and had spent all that she had; and she was no better, but rather grew worse. She had heard about Jesus, and came up behind him in the crowd and touched his cloak, for she said, 'If I but touch his clothes, I will be made well.'*

Desperation for healing and the search for miracle cures is nothing new. Jesus encountered it everywhere. The desperation of a parent, the desperation of a woman, and not enough time to meet the needs of the crowds. The woman here is ground down, willing herself into invisibility. Her illness has led others to avoid her for fear of contamination, and she does not see herself worthy of even asking for healing. The stigma of chronic illness has slowly erased her from her community.

Jesus heals her – but he heals much more than her body: he sees her and makes her seen. He restores her in the sight of others and affirms her faith. She not just another human being, she is worthy of his love, his attention, his care. Therein lies her healing – and the challenge to a crowd that ignored her.

Prayer

Loving God, open our eyes today to one person whom we have failed to see, or hear, or treat as made in your image, and show us how to share the depth of your love for them. Amen.

Tuesday, Week 3
SHIELDING THE VULNERABLE

Read: Mark 5.35-43

> *Then Jesus put them all outside, and took the child's father and mother and those who were with him, and went in where the child was. He took her by the hand and said to her, 'Talitha cum', which means, 'Little girl, get up!' And immediately the girl got up and began to walk about ...*

Jairus could not be more different from the woman with haemorrhages. He has status, power and wealth. We know his name.

He asks Jesus to heal his daughter.

The crowds are interested: the woman was of little consequence, but a high-profile healing makes a good spectacle. The woman was under-seen, Jairus is over-seen. He does not need more attention, more status, but less.

Jesus had healed the woman in public and made the crowd see her. Here, he does the opposite. He sends people away and gives the family privacy and dignity in their pain. Jairus had needs too; the crowd ignored them as they ignored the woman's. Jesus sees and responds to both.

Consequently, he challenges the crowd's perception of who matters: they both do – woman and man, rich and poor, known and unknown. They are made in the image of God, precious, loved, and worthy of time, care and kindness.

Prayer

Loving God, we pray for the great and the small in human eyes, that we may learn to see them as equally made in your image and in need of your embrace. Amen.

LEARNING FROM THE OTHER

Read: Luke 10.25-37

> 'Teacher,' he said, 'what must I do to inherit eternal life?' Jesus said to him, 'What is written in the law? What do you read there?' He answered, 'You shall love the Lord your God with all your heart, and with all your soul, and with all your strength, and with all your mind; and your neighbour as yourself.'

Jesus' teaching of loving our neighbour has always been a sticking point. It's easy to find reasons why we can't do it, why it is unreasonable, or to deny someone is our neighbour. This is exactly what happens in the parable of the Good Samaritan. It is somewhat easy to say, of course, the neighbour is the despised Samaritan, so we must all be as good as he is.

But this isn't all that the parable is saying. The man's question was, 'Who is my neighbour?' The answer: the Samaritan. The man is invited to identify, not with the Samaritan, but with the beaten and broken Jewish man. If we follow this logic, we are invited to think of ourselves, not as the saviours of those who are hurt, but as those who are hurt and in need of tending by and learning from those we despise, disregard and, possibly, oppress.

Prayer

God of challenge and transformation, open our hearts to learn from those we would rather walk past, ignore or silence, and see your face as we look into theirs. Amen.

EQUALS BEFORE GOD

Read: Luke 18.9-14

> 'The Pharisee, standing by himself, was praying thus, "God, I thank you that I am not like other people: thieves, rogues, adulterers, or even like this tax-collector. I fast twice a week; I give a tenth of all my income." But the tax-collector, standing far off, would not even look up to heaven, but was beating his breast and saying, "God, be merciful to me, a sinner!" '

Luke 18 contrasts those who think they know how to be good with those who do not. The Pharisee prides himself on his practice of justice – giving money away, fasting. All good things, but he practises these as a way to make himself worthy, rather than as a response to God's grace. When justice leads to pride and superiority, it excludes and diminishes others.

The tax-collector knows himself to be unjust, in need of God: his pursuit of justice can make space for others, equally inadequate and needing God. He belongs to a fellowship of grace, within which all others are invited. The Pharisee sees himself as part of a select fellowship of striving and purity from which those who do not measure up are excluded and treated as less worthy. How can we pursue justice in ways that makes space for all at the table?

Prayer

Gracious God, we thank you that you take our feeble efforts and transform them in your mercy; help us work together as a fellowship of grace to see justice bloom among us. Amen.

HUMANISING THE OTHER

Read: John 8.1-11

> ❝ *When they kept on questioning him, he straightened up and said to them, 'Let anyone among you who is without sin be the first to throw a stone at her.' And once again he bent down and wrote on the ground. When they heard it, they went away, one by one, beginning with the elders.* ❞

It is easy to reduce justice to rules and principles, and forget real, complicated people, with their history and relationships.

But if real people disappear, justice does too. If we turn people into caricatures, fail to understand their journey, and how others have shaped their choices, justice fails. Here, Pharisees shame a woman caught in adultery, and quote the rules.

It isn't that rules don't matter – Jesus makes that clear when he tells her to 'sin no more'. But he sees a whole person, brought alone for a crime that can only be committed jointly. His response forces the Pharisees to see themselves as equal to the woman: sinners needing grace. The woman is humanised, by being treated with grace, and by being held responsible for her life going forward. The Pharisees are humanised, too – no longer faceless, perfect judges, but fellow fallible humans. True justice is a meeting of persons.

Prayer

Loving God, help us see the face and the life of those we like to condemn for their failings. Give us the grace to hold together accountability and mercy. Amen.

CONTAGIOUS HOLINESS

Read: Mark 2.13-22

> *When the scribes of the Pharisees saw that he was eating with sinners and tax-collectors, they said to his disciples, 'Why does he eat with tax-collectors and sinners?' When Jesus heard this, he said to them, 'Those who are well have no need of a physician, but those who are sick; I have come to call not the righteous but sinners.'*

There is a paradox at the heart of doing justice. To do justice needs passion, fire, a keen sense of injustice and compassion for those who suffer. Yet deep passion easily leads to new forms of injustice, as those who disagree or lag behind are excluded, criticised and caricatured as uncaring or evil.

One answer is to understand ourselves as part of this fellowship of grace, which prevents us ever thinking of ourselves as superior. Another is to follow the model of Jesus. As sin was often treated as contagious, 'good' people refused to eat with 'sinners'. Human beings have a tendency to separate themselves from those whose words, lifestyles or beliefs they despise or disagree with. Yet Jesus did the exact opposite. Instead of treating sin as contagious, he practiced contagious holiness: a love so profound, that it inevitably drew the other into new life and relationship.

Prayer

Holy God, we are both inspired and fearful before your holiness; may you transform our hearts, that we become people whose holiness and justice are expressed in contagious love and grace. Amen.

JUSTICE IN THE SHAPE OF A CROSS

No matter what laws and guidance are given to human beings, they struggle to do justly and love mercy. It is only in Jesus that justice and mercy are perfectly united – in one perfect life, a sacrificial death and glorious resurrection.

Action for the week

Justice is costly. What one thing could you pledge to do to love your neighbour more deeply than you have chosen to do so far? Try and think of something personal, which brings you in contact with a real person.

BREAKING DOWN BARRIERS

Read: Luke 4.16-29

> *Jesus stood up to read, and the scroll of the prophet Isaiah was given to him ... 'The Spirit of the Lord is upon me, because he has anointed me to bring good news to the poor. He has sent me to proclaim release to the captives and recovery of sight to the blind, to let the oppressed go free, to proclaim the year of the Lord's favour.'*

This is good news, right? Freedom, release and God's favour: what more can we possibly want? Jesus' listeners agree – to start with.

They agree with the good stuff, and they imagine themselves receiving the good stuff. They thought of themselves as oppressed by the Romans, being promised release.

But Jesus starts his ministry by confounding expectations. To start with, he omits the final line from Isaiah, the one promising vengeance. Then, he talks of Elijah and Elisha's miracles – miracles of healing for Gentiles! These people's world is set upside down: vengeance denied, and blessing extended to those they despise. The promise of justice and restoration is one that suffers no barriers: it is extended to all, and the barriers that try and hoard blessings are shattered.

What barriers do you think you put around your views of who should be blessed?

Prayer

Lord Jesus, you came and brought down barriers that divide humanity: help us seek justice together and for one another today, regardless of our human differences. Amen.

FROM SCARCITY TO ABUNDANCE:
FEEDING THE HUNGRY

Read: Mark 6.30-44

> *Taking the five loaves and the two fish, he looked up to heaven, and blessed and broke the loaves, and gave them to his disciples to set before the people; and he divided the two fish among them all. And all ate and were filled; and they took up twelve baskets full of broken pieces and of the fish.*

There is little more basic than bread. If you have access to the staple food of your culture, you live. If you do not, you starve. Bread is a measure of justice. Those who hoard it deprive those who need it, and waste it themselves. Bread reminds us that justice and injustice are practical, embodied, and urgent. As the people of God moved away from Sinai, the memory of manna in the desert became distant. God's abundance was forgotten and scarcity led to competition for resources and increasing inequalities of wealth.

In the midst of scarcity, of worry about providing for the crowd, Jesus proclaims anew that God's abundance is still there to be received. The meal is simple, but everyone has their fill, and leftovers are taken away – enough for those who were absent, through choice or necessity.

Where are the 'leftovers' in your life? Love, food, resources to be shared?

Prayer

Generous God, give us today our daily bread, and let us not hoard for tomorrow the bread that our neighbour needs today. Amen.

FROM SCARCITY TO ABUNDANCE: THE FIRST BANQUET

Read: Mark 6.14-29

> *But an opportunity came when Herod on his birthday gave a banquet for his courtiers and officers and for the leaders of Galilee. When his daughter Herodias came in and danced, she pleased Herod and his guests; and the king said to the girl, 'Ask me for whatever you wish, and I will give it.'*

The feeding of the five thousand is a high point in Jesus' ministry. So high it is easy to forget it comes after a very low point. Side-by-side in Mark 6 are two banquets. One, gathered around Jesus, where all are invited, all are fed simply and abundantly, and leftovers bless even more people. A banquet where the king himself is host and servant.

The other banquet is Herod's, a very different king. Food and surroundings are luxurious; only a select few are invited. Herod's banquet may be lavish, but it is marked by scarcity: lack of grace, lack of guests, lack of inclusion, lack of leftovers. Instead of finishing with shared abundance, it ends with the murder of John the Baptist. Herod had much, but wanted more.

The choice is stark: which king would we prefer to follow? What does that mean for our choices of food, friends and surroundings?

Prayer

Generous God, help us not be so ground down by the world around us or enamoured with our own importance that we fail to see your offer of simple and generous abundance. Amen.

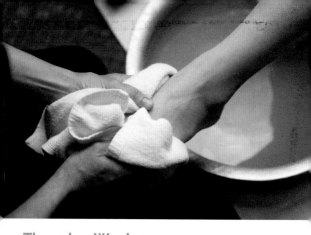

WASHING FEET

Read: John 13.1-20

> ❝ Jesus got up from the table, took off his outer robe, and tied a towel around himself. Then he poured water into a basin and began to wash the disciples' feet and to wipe them with the towel that was tied around him. ❞

The scene of Jesus washing his disciples' feet is both strangely familiar, and strangely foreign. We no longer wash feet when entering a house as a routine action. It is easy to forget that this was a menial job, that of a servant, woman or child, and occasionally a mark of special honour for an important guest.

Jesus, the most powerful, important person in the room, shatters expectations. He not only washes the disciples' feet, he washes the feet of the disciple who will betray him and of the one who will deny him. Betrayal and denial loom large in Jesus' words. Yet he washes their feet, treats them with honour, affirms their humanity together with their need of God. Even where guilt and sin abound, Jesus reminds his people of their profound dignity and belovedness.

What kind of justice is this?

Prayer

Loving God, we thank you that in all your power, you are willing to kneel and wash us clean: help us remember this when we are tempted to diminish, dismiss or condemn another human being. Amen.

IN BETWEEN CRIMINALS

Read: Luke 23.26-43

> *'We indeed have been condemned justly, for we are getting what we deserve for our deeds, but this man has done nothing wrong.' Then [the criminal] said, 'Jesus, remember me when you come into your kingdom.' He replied, 'Truly I tell you, today you will be with me in Paradise.'*

Jesus' politics of generosity and compassion did not just change the lives of individuals, they challenged the system that denied them dignity, love and forgiveness, and thereby sustained an oppressive and immovable order. Jesus and empire could not co-exist, so that, in the end, those with power – over political, religious and personal empires – united to get rid of him.

The justice system, meant to protect the vulnerable, is so perverted that even Pilate recognises they are putting an innocent man to death. The complete failure of human justice is graphically depicted as Jesus hangs between two known criminals.

Yet in the midst of desolation, Jesus keeps practising life-changing compassion, and reaches out with grace to the criminal who asks for it. The man is guilty and will still die, but just deserts are not the end of the road. Compassion reaches beyond justice, and makes all things new.

Prayer

Just and merciful God, soften our hearts, that where we have power and build little empires of our own, we may be moved and changed by compassion. Amen.

THE **FOOLISHNESS OF THE CROSS**

Read: 1 Corinthians 1.18-31

> *We proclaim Christ crucified, a stumbling-block to Jews and foolishness to Gentiles, but to those who are the called, both Jews and Greeks, Christ the power of God and the wisdom of God. For God's foolishness is wiser than human wisdom, and God's weakness is stronger than human strength.*

Paul's words are stark: the cross makes no sense to the way humans normally think, within a culture of inequality, competition for resources and fear. The cross is foolish, because grace is illogical. Grace is patently un-just, completely underserved, it does not try to guarantee the future, it is freely offered with no ties, and cannot be imposed. If God loves justice and God's revelation of himself in Jesus focuses on grace, then justice and grace must belong together.

Grace goes against our deepest human instincts to protect ourselves and reach for retribution. 'An eye for an eye' had curbed revenge and established proportionality. In Jesus, the logic of escalating revenge is not merely restrained, but turned into escalating forgiveness, as Jesus tells his disciples to forgive seventy times seven times. Grace transforms the justice of scarcity, anxiety and fear, which only considers what one deserves or is entitled to, into generosity, gift, and hope.

Prayer

Merciful God, help us share the good news of forgiveness, grace and new beginnings in our words and relationships, that follow in your way of grace. Amen.

DO THIS TO REMEMBER ME

The God of Scripture invites us to be holy, as he is holy, and holiness and justice walk together. But holiness is not something that simply happens. It is practised until it becomes habit. And one of the practices that shape us for justice as a church is that of Communion.

Action for the week

This week, every time you eat bread, place a donation in a basket to be taken to a local foodbank. Every time you drink wine (or tea, or coffee) set aside money to be given to a clean water/sanitation project abroad.

LIFE-SHAPING STORIES

Read: Luke 22.7-23

> Then he took a cup, and after giving thanks he said, 'Take this and divide it among yourselves; for I tell you that from now on I will not drink of the fruit of the vine until the kingdom of God comes.' Then he took a loaf of bread, and when he had given thanks, he broke it and gave it to them, saying, 'This is my body, which is given for you. Do this in remembrance of me.'

Scripture holds deep wisdom about humanity. From the early times of the people's Exodus from Egypt, they were told to remember the stories and the reasons for the stories. To help them remember, they were given words and actions to perform together. When you learn a sport, or a musical instrument, you develop muscle memory, which takes over so you do not need to think about what you need to do. In the words and actions we repeat in worship, we develop spiritual and ethical memory that can sustain and shape our lives.

The instructions about Holy Communion give a pattern for the life of the community: gather together, share a simple meal between equals, between companions, as all eat and drink of the same simple fare, gathered around Jesus. How can this 'muscle memory' shape our lives more widely?

Prayer

Lord Jesus, may we remember you through our worship, our daily words and actions, our choices and attitudes: form us into your likeness as we share our lives as your people. Amen.

THIS IS MY BODY

Read: James 2.1-17

> *What good is it, my brothers and sisters, if you say you have faith but do not have works? Can faith save you? If a brother or sister is naked and lacks daily food, and one of you says to them, 'Go in peace; keep warm and eat your fill', and yet you do not supply their bodily needs, what is the good of that? So faith by itself, if it has no works, is dead.*

The most obvious thing about Holy Communion – yet perhaps something we rarely reflect on – is how physical it is. It invites us to partake in bread and wine. Both are symbols of life – bread as a staple, wine as safe hydration in places with poor sanitation. Their absence is almost always a sign of inequality, and hoarding them forms the beginning of injustice. To have bread and wine at the centre of worship proclaims that bodies matter, and feeding bodies matters. We cannot be a just or holy community unless we examine what we do with our material resources, and how this affects those around us.

In addition, Communion requires us to share bread and wine: justice can never be served in isolation, it is always relational. In Communion, we respond to the call of equality and justice in our practical, economic relationships. The question is, how is that reflected beyond our worship?

Prayer

Righteous God, we pray that every time we eat this bread and drink this cup, we would commit ourselves to your vision of justice and care for all humanity. Amen.

'DISCERNING THE BODY'

Read: 1 Corinthians 11.23-34

> *Whoever, therefore, eats the bread or drinks the cup of the Lord in an unworthy manner will be answerable for the body and blood of the Lord. Examine yourselves, and only then eat of the bread and drink of the cup. For all who eat and drink without discerning the body, eat and drink judgement against themselves.*

Paul has sharp words for the Corinthian church. Holy Communion cannot be celebrated without self-awareness of the state of the body of Christ, the church. Communion is not simply about a vertical relationship with God, but about how that relationship is worked out in practice: do the relationships between members of the church actually reflect the radical care and equality that we proclaim through our symbolic actions?

Discerning the body cannot simply be about a local gathering of the like-minded. Who is missing from the Christians who do assemble, left out, unseen or unwanted? Are some Christians separating themselves from another church down the road? Paul's words prompt penetrating and uncomfortable questions about the choices we make, and how we relate to Christians and churches beyond our doors, in a vastly unequal world, and about our responsibility towards them, and theirs towards us.

Prayer

All-seeing God, teach to see the Body as you see the Body: never to ignore, dismiss or exclude any of your people but accept that we hold bread and wine in common with all your children. Amen.

THE PRACTICE OF TRUTH-TELLING

Read: Isaiah 59.1-15

> *Our transgressions indeed are with us, and we know our iniquities: transgressing, and denying the Lord, and turning away from following our God … Justice is turned back, and righteousness stands at a distance; for truth stumbles in the public square, and uprightness cannot enter.*

Discerning the body goes hand-in-hand with honesty. In most churches, Holy Communion is preceded by a time of confession. Confession is an invitation to truth-telling, to acknowledge our need of God's salvation in every possible area of our lives.

In practice, however, confession is often reduced to those things we do that we have the power not to do, or do differently. But the truth of our humanity goes far beyond this. It encompasses those things we have no power over: the systems we are part of and condone or profit from. If we confess our sins together, then our truth-telling has to be more than the sum of our individual sin and brokenness. Confession together is an invitation to acknowledge the brokenness, injustice and sin of the world and its systems, of our nations, our churches and communities, and asking God to lead us into better ways.

Prayer

God of all truth, show us the things we would rather ignore in our lives, soften our hearts, and lead us into newness of life. Amen.

HE OPENED WIDE HIS ARMS UPON THE CROSS

Read: Matthew 26.20-45

> Then Jesus went with them to a place called Gethsemane; and he said to his disciples, 'Sit here while I go over there and pray.' ... And going a little farther, he threw himself on the ground and prayed, 'My Father, if it is possible, let this cup pass from me; yet not what I want but what you want.'

Holy Communion gathers together the entire story, and retells it through words and actions. It is uncompromisingly truthful about the reality of sin and injustice, and the cost of dealing with them.

Communion proclaims that the body of Christ was broken, and it is only through that brokenness that we can be gathered in truth and justice. The practice of Communion is a clear safeguard against triumphalism, or the kind of heroism that seeks to overcome injustice through sheer power.

Communion shapes us for justice because it reminds us, again and again, that the way of justice goes through the cross.

As we are sent out, at the end of a service, to 'love and serve the Lord', it is a call to go, not in our own strength, but a call to follow Christ and his example of costly compassion.

Prayer

God of the cross, we pray for the courage to follow you, and the desire to want to follow you when shadows gather and the way of justice is costly. Amen.

COMMUNION AS A GLIMPSE OF THE KINGDOM

Read: Luke 24.13-35

> When he was at the table with them, he took bread, blessed and broke it, and gave it to them. Then their eyes were opened, and they recognized him; and he vanished from their sight. They said to each other, 'Were not our hearts burning within us while he was talking to us on the road, while he was opening the scriptures to us?'

Holy Communion calls us to deep encounter with the Risen Christ, whose earthly life and death are not the final word, and whose resurrection makes his presence possible with us. Just like the disciples on the Emmaus road, we are invited to let Scripture and the breaking of the bread interrupt our present and reshape our direction of travel. As we encounter Christ, our hearts are inevitably directed towards the world he came to save.

And as we seek to love as Jesus did, the very words and actions of Communion, with their radical call to equality and justice, challenge us to interrogate our lives within and without the community of faith. As Michael Ramsey once wrote, 'The supreme question is not what we make of the Eucharist, but what the Eucharist is making of us, as together with the Word of God it fashions us into the way of Christ.'

Prayer

Risen Christ, may we know your presence on the way, and let ourselves be fashioned into a people of truth, compassion and justice in our words, deeds and relationships. Amen.

WALKING THROUGH HOLY WEEK

As we walk through Holy Week, we pay attention to the interweaving of justice and mercy in Jesus' words and action, from the triumph of his arrival to his death on the cross.

Action for the week

This week, spend time considering a situation of injustice, at home or abroad, you particularly care about. How can you come alongside those suffering and hear their stories? What one thing could you do express practical support?

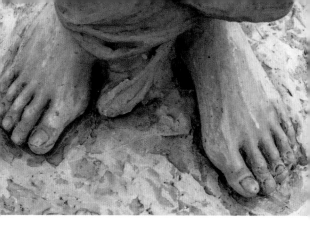

AT THE FEET OF JESUS

Read: John 12.1-11

> Mary took a pound of costly perfume made of pure nard, anointed Jesus' feet, and wiped them with her hair. The house was filled with the fragrance of the perfume.
> But Judas Iscariot, one of his disciples (the one who was about to betray him), said, 'Why was this perfume not sold for three hundred denarii and the money given to the poor?'

The tyranny of scarcity reaches deep. Even seeking justice can become ruled by productivity and efficiency and overlook the Sabbath principle: there is more than needed, life is not a zero-sum game. Judas instrumentalises and perverts justice, and forgets that giving to God and giving to our neighbour are not in competition, but belong together.

Judas' fake care, from a position of authority sitting at the table, contrasts with Mary's selfless devotion, despite not having a space at the table. Mary's status may be lower, a woman, expected to serve, but she is the first person to wash feet in Holy Week, with perfume and her own hair for a towel.

Mary's care for the person and body of Jesus reminds us that seeking justice goes deeper than words and activism. It cuts to the heart of our relationship with God. Loving God and neighbour are two sides of the same coin.

Prayer

Generous God, help us never treat others as a problem or a project, but only ever come alongside in humility and shared humanity. Amen.

Tuesday of Holy Week

WHOEVER SERVES ME MUST FOLLOW ME

Read: John 12.20-33

> *Jesus said, 'Very truly, I tell you, unless a grain of wheat falls into the earth and dies, it remains just a single grain; but if it dies, it bears much fruit. Those who love their life lose it, and those who hate their life in this world will keep it for eternal life.'*

Holy Week gets progressively darker. And threaded through its events come Jesus' words highlighting betrayal, denial and the cost of walking in the ways of God. The logic of the kingdom jars with earthly logic. Why should death lead to life? Why should loving one's life lead to losing it? It seems unfair. Ahead of the cross, Jesus explains the logic of the cross, foolish to bystanders.

There is no Christian path to salvation that does not go through the cross: no fullness of life, no justice, no renewal of all things. I wonder what the disciples made of it?

It is easier with the benefit of hindsight and knowledge of the resurrection. But even today, the road towards justice and mercy is often uncertain, full of fear and anxiety. Yet the call is the same: to walk the way of the cross, keeping our eyes on Jesus and his promise of eternal life.

Prayer

Lord Jesus, help us discern the way ahead, and cling to you rather than our own strength and life, that we may see your salvation. Amen.

Wednesday of Holy Week

JUST AS I HAVE LOVED YOU

Read: John 13.21-35

> *Jesus said, 'I give you a new commandment, that you love one another. Just as I have loved you, you also should love one another. By this everyone will know that you are my disciples, if you have love for one another.'*

The theme of sacrifice persists throughout the lead up to Good Friday. Here, Jesus begins to wrap up his teaching to his disciples with a constant heartbeat: love one another. This love has texture, depth and challenge. Jesus' words on love are immediately preceded by the reality of the betrayal to come. None of the disciples understood what Judas' role was going to be. Nor did they foresee that they themselves would desert Jesus. Yet they are told to love one another – with no exceptions.

This is where the instructions bite: it would be much easier to do justice if we could simply give those we dislike what we think they deserve. The Gospel, however, does not allow us this luxury. Jesus' call is for a group of less-than-perfect disciples to learn to love one another as he had loved them – through the way of the cross.

Prayer

Loving God, create in us the desire to love as you have loved, so that we may love one another as your people, and share this love with all we encounter. Amen.

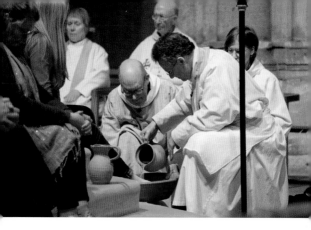

Maundy Thursday
LETTING OUR FEET BE WASHED

Read: John 13.1-17

> *After Jesus had washed their feet, had put on his robe, and had returned to the table, he said to them, 'Do you know what I have done to you? You call me Teacher and Lord – and you are right, for that is what I am. So if I, your Lord and Teacher, have washed your feet, you also ought to wash one another's feet.'*

On Maundy Thursday, we again come to an account of washing of feet. Mary had spontaneously anointed Jesus' feet with perfume, acknowledging Jesus' infinite worth and belovedness. Her actions heighten the significance of the scene that now unfolds. Peter argues with Jesus that he should wash Jesus' feet, with water and a towel, in response to Jesus' intention to wash the disciples' feet.

Jesus places himself on a par with those – normally ignored – who wash the feet of others. Peter is trying to restore the normal social order. Jesus firmly challenges it.

Peter needs his own feet washed – his view of the world, his hierarchising of people, needs transforming, so that he stands with others in a fellowship of grace. The disciples cannot work towards transformation unless they are first transformed. They cannot work towards transformation from a place of superiority – only as fellow human beings, equally sinful, and equally beloved.

Prayer

Lord Jesus, we lay down our pride and ideas of superiority before you: wash us clean, and renew our minds and imaginations that we may follow you more truly. Amen.

A STRANGE KIND OF KING

Read: John 19.1-30

> Carrying the cross by himself, Jesus went out to what is called The Place of the Skull, which in Hebrew is called Golgotha. There they crucified him, and with him two others, one on either side, with Jesus between them. Pilate also had an inscription written and put on the cross. It read, 'Jesus of Nazareth, the King of the Jews.'

Throughout Jesus' trial and execution he is accused of claiming kingship, mocked as a false king, charged as a king. Who could look less like a king than a poor itinerant preacher brutalised by Roman and Jewish leaders?

Surrounded by great and powerful men – kings after a fashion – Jesus experiences the abuse and perversion of justice that so many endured then and too many suffer today. All too often the powerful justify their actions and choices, while the powerless suffer in silence.

God incarnate – more powerful than them all – chooses to embody a different way to justice, a different way to be king. He identifies with the powerless, and takes upon himself the cost of injustice, and of challenging it. The mustard seed of the kingdom is ready to bloom, against the expectations of those gathered to watch.

Prayer

God of the powerless, help us see where you are at work, challenging and reshaping people and systems, and to join in with your work of justice and renewal. Amen.

Easter Eve

WHEN INJUSTICE SEEMS TO TRIUMPH

Read: Matthew 27.57-66

> *Joseph took the body and wrapped it in a clean linen cloth and laid it in his own new tomb, which he had hewn in the rock. He then rolled a great stone to the door of the tomb and went away. Mary Magdalene and the other Mary were there, sitting opposite the tomb.*

Holy Saturday is a quiet day. A day for silent despair in face of the triumph of death, of injustice, of all the forces of evil and the human beings who side with them. It is a day for lament at the brokenness of the world, and the cost of challenging the status quo.

We know that Easter is coming. But the resurrection does not take away the cross or its scars. Much of the world still lives on Holy Saturday, poised between the pain of the cross and the hope of resurrection. Today we weep with those who weep, and sit with those who have no tears left to cry. We rage at injustice and the way it so often seems to triumph.

Today, with all of creation, we cry out 'Lord, have mercy', and wait for God to meet us in pain and despair, and lead us into a future we can barely imagine.

Prayer

Lord, have mercy.
Christ, have mercy.
Lord, have mercy.

Easter Day
A NEW
VOCATION

Easter Day
A NEW VOCATION

Read: John 21.1-19

> *Jesus said to them, 'Come and have breakfast.' Now none of the disciples dared to ask him, Who are you?' because they knew it was the Lord.*

Resurrection is hard to believe. It was much easier for the disciples to return to something solid, concrete and familiar, life as they knew it – fishing. It is hard to know what to do with something completely new. What did they talk about as they fished? The puzzle of the resurrection? Or shame that they had not stayed with Jesus, or even denied him? How do you pick up the threads of life, old or new, with the heavy burden of a broken relationship?

Going back is not an option. Jesus cooks for them on the beach, caring first for their bodies, reminding them of his promise of abundance, of feeding the hungry. But they cannot simply go forward. The past looms too large. Truth is needed before restoration; love and justice must walk hand-in-hand. So Jesus reminds Peter of his threefold betrayal, by asking three times, 'do you love me?' Peter must confront the past to walk freely into a better future. His new vocation – to feed Jesus' lambs – rests, not on his strength and success, but on his acknowledgement of failure, and experience of grace received. And there lies the heart of the Gospel.

As you move into a time of remembering the resurrection, where do you think your own calling lies?

Who might you be called to feed?

Prayer

God of grace and mercy, we rejoice at your presence with us, and bring to you the whole of our lives that you may shine light in the shadows. May we walk in grace and hope as we share the good news of your resurrection. Amen.

GOING FURTHER

Jesus Christ is at the heart of our vision for the Church of England.

Where will a life centred on Christ take you?

We hope you have enjoyed this #LiveLent journey. Here are some ways you might want to travel further in the faith in the days and month ahead:

Join with others in worship and service at your local church. Find thousands of services and events, groups and activities taking place both on site and on line near you via AChurchNearYou.com

Sign up for future Church of England reflections. Visit churchofengland.org to sign up for future campaigns and resources – including Advent and Christmas reflections. It's free to sign up for emails and you can easily opt out at any time.

Explore God in everyday life with *Everyday Faith*. *Everyday Faith* provide resources for individuals and churches to help them find and follow God in everyday life – including prayers, reflections and stories. Visit churchofengland.org/everyday-faith to find out more.

Take part in *Thy Kingdom Come*. *Thy Kingdom Come* is a global prayer movement inviting Christians to pray during the nine days between Ascension and Pentecost for more people to come to know Jesus Christ. Find out more at thykingdomcome.global.